G000131358

Dedicated to Fran Ford

ONCE UPON A CHINA

CJ Lim + Steve McCloy

Routledge
Taylor & Francis Group

LONDON AND NEW YORK

First published 2021
by Routledge
2 Park Square, Milton Park, Abingdon, Oxon, OX14 4RN
and by Routledge
52 Vanderbilt Avenue, New York, NY 10017

Routledge is an imprint of the Taylor & Francis Group, an informa business

British Library Cataloguing-in-Publication Data
A catalogue record for this book is available from the British Library

Library of Congress Cataloging-in-Publication Data
Names: Lim, C. J., author. | McCloy, Steve, author.
Title: Once upon a China / CJ Lim & Steve McCloy.
Description: Abingdon, Oxon ; New York, NY : Routledge, 2021. | Includes bibliographical references and index.
Identifiers: LCCN 2020041488 (print) | LCCN 2020041489 (ebook) | ISBN 9781138224414 (hbk) | ISBN 9781138224438 (pbk) | ISBN 9781315402543 (ebk)
Subjects: LCSH: Architecture--China--Themes, motives. | Architecture--China--Comic books, strips, etc.
Classification: LCC NA1540 .L537 2021 (print) | LCC NA1540 (ebook) | DDC 720.951--dc23
LC record available at https://lccn.loc.gov/2020041488
LC ebook record available at https://lccn.loc.gov/2020041489

ISBN: 978-1-138-22441-4 (hbk)
ISBN: 978-1-138-22443-8 (pbk)
ISBN: 978-1-315-40254-3 (ebk)

Printed and bound in Great Britain by
TJ Books Limited, Padstow, Cornwall

Contents

PREFACE

'**O**nce Upon a Time...' is the threshold by which we enter a narrative past. A closer translation of the typical Chinese story opening 很久很久以前 is 'a very, very long time ago'. The time travelled into the past is of course totally ambiguous in stories, as is the requirement for the narrative to speak of true real-life events. Tales passed down by the spoken word and re-writing are subject to degradation of their empirical evidence – versions of events carried between generations are shaped, textured and coloured by their consecutive bearers, and inevitably begin transforming into legends or myths. These Chinese 'whispers' should primarily be explored through empathy and imagination. History is contaminated with seductive and narcissistic assertions, shadows, lies and age-old deceptions. It is also seasoned and spiced by bizarre and idiosyncratic customs and cultural activities, and by stories of great beauty, honour and sadness.

During the Cultural Revolution from 1966 until 1976, the Communist Party of China (CPC) ordered a bibliocaust, the mandatory burning of books. Mao Zedong, the chairman of the party, deemed that the majority of literary works were 'poisonous weeds' and the drastic actions were intended to destroy the legacy of feudal and capitalist narratives, clearing the fields of independent thoughts for the planting of a newly constructed collective ideology. 'There is no revolution like the Communist revolution. You simply burn all the books, kill all the thinking people and use the poor proletariat to create a very simple benchmark to gauge social change.'[1] More than four decades later, books are migrating back into households and libraries all across the country. Preoccupied by alternative ideas of Chinese living, Ou Ning, the activist, artist and curator, is confident that bringing a branch of Nanjing's Librairie Avant-Garde to the rural Bishan would be a key ingredient for his utopian artistic commune: 'Today, bookstores are far more popular than museums in China's cities. Chinese people are more interested in books than art. A book might be helpful for their job or education, and there is a strong cultural belief that books can change your life.'[2]

Bookstore frenzy is part of a 21st century capitalist phenomenon that has not been lost on China. Thousands of fans would form huge lines and even camp outside stores in time for the release of new titles in the 'Harry Potter' or 'Hunger Games' series. Some Chinese students read the Potter stories to improve their English, translating every unfamiliar word by using a dictionary with their friends.[3] But this hunger pales into insignificance compared to that for the first shipments of Western classics following the Cultural Revolution. Author Yu Hua, still a child in the late 1970s, recalls the excitement and the queueing that was required just to enter the bookstore, and ultimately the disappointment of those (including himself) who were too late: 'We would gather around somebody we knew and enviously reach out a hand to touch their reprints of Anna Karenina, Le Père Goriot, and David Copperfield. Having lived so long in reading famine, we found it a matchless pleasure just to feast our eyes on the new covers of these classics. Some generously held the books up to our noses and let us sniff their subtle, inky smell. For me that odour was a heady scent.'[4]

In China, 'Dream of the Red Mansion', 'Journey to the West', 'The Water Margin', and 'Romance of the Three Kingdoms' are regarded as the Four Great Classic Novels. These seminal pre-modern fictions are extensively read, from scholars to governing rulers, and contain diverse voices and philosophical perspectives on history as well as satires that have defined past developments of Chinese societies and politics. Fiction has not always enjoyed high status in traditional China, as a result of 'moral and aesthetic judgements rather than a political one'.[5] The Tang dynasty marks the era in which scholars first came to distinguish fiction from history, and the narratives were some of the earliest examples of storytelling employed to achieve social change in China. During the literary inquisition of the Manchus, all works containing anti-dynastic sentiment were comprehensively destroyed. Confucian themes of loyalty, filial piety, chastity and righteousness, played a role of unquestioned importance in the development of Chinese fiction, but the situation changed – storytelling started to make the readers question their own lives, which included 'the practise of consulting an astrologer in matters of betrothal, employing match-makers in arranged marriages, the demands made on women, the excessive emphasis placed on having a male heir, the privileges of the upper classes, and other inequities inherent in the social system'.[6]

Storytelling has always had great power, and writing can spread empathy and ideas like no other medium. This is clearly demonstrated by the ideas gleaned from the writings of Confucius and Karl Marx – the foundations for many of China's political structures and personal belief systems. There recalls a time where the only books anyone had in China were unopened box-sets of Mao's collected writings, and the 'Little Red Book' (1964). During the Cultural Revolution, the Communist Party of China printed an estimated five billion copies of the 'Little Red Book', over 500 editions and 50 languages – considering a total world population of around four billion in 1976 that equates to more than enough copies for each and every living man, woman and child on the planet. The principled texts sought to energise the poor into having a common aim for a utopian world, and a world-wide Marxist-Leninist victory, but recognised that contradictions would need to be faced with struggle and war. Mao prepared the ground for modern China, but just as in George Orwell's 'Nineteen Eighty-Four' (1949), he instilled the dogma and belief that eternal peace meant eternal war.

For scholars of China, it is pertinent to understand the power that Mao attributed not just to literature but also to comics and cartoons, having claimed that their widespread effect on peasants was akin to a population where everyone had been through 'political school'![7] If only architectural drawings could employ similar humour, critique and storytelling, then they too might have significant relevance and effectiveness! In 'Once Upon a China', comics is the unorthodox but extraordinary medium for architectural speculations, the communication of design intent and the understanding of how urban form and its infrastructures affect our daily lives. The eccentric characteristics of comics enriches the process of conception and conceptualisation of design – the fragmented yet sequential nature proves versatile in the imagination of spatial experiences, enabling the complex story of the place, brief and building to materialise gradually, perhaps even gaining a delightful and surprising sense of continuous drama as spaces unfold. At the same time, the politicisation of architecture through comics would offer the coming generations of Chinese architects the critical thinking to reimagine the urban condition beyond the exuberance of non-contextual Western capitalist models.

'Once Upon a China' is an architectural story with exploratory spirit and emotions, and each chapter is conceived as a specific theme of Chinese identity – domesticity, consumerism, democracy and adaptability. Correspondingly, 'Dream of the Red Mansion', 'Journey to the West', 'Water Margin', and 'Romance of the Three Kingdoms' are employed to provide the humanity and poetic design stimulus for each of the case studies to re-evaluate and empathise with the nation's identity – its different forms, its collective phenomena, and its fragility, freedom and limitation. Whether it is reconstructing an identity from the past, or importing from external sources, or adapting to the unexpected conditions of a future environment to identify new forms of architecture and urbanism, the narratives of the chapters are intricately linked. 'Adaptability' focuses on the resilience of communities and the environment in the age of rampant 'Consumerism'. 'Democracy' seeks to situate itself within sustainable policies and politics to adapt society, economy and the city. 'Domesticity' rekindles the optimism of the home-front and humanity in citizens who are pessimistic about relentless urbanisation and inequality, and the weight of material excess.

There is undoubtedly a synergy between the medium of comics and the city as a living organism of diverse identities. The editors of 'Comics and the City: Urban Space in Print, Picture and Sequence' (2010), Jörn Ahrens and Arno Meteling, emphasise how comics 'specifically urban topoi, self-portraits, forms of cultural memorizing, and variant readings of the city have special competences for capturing urban space and city life, and representing it aesthetically because of their hybrid nature consisting of words, pictures, and sequences'.[8] In the real and the imagined inhabitation of urban environments, 'comics and other forms of popular media have circled back to the pulp magazine imagery of early science fiction in search of striking new ways to represent the directions our society is taking. In some cases, they do so to regain some of the giddy excitement about the world of tomorrow'.[9] The comic-inspired drawings in this book seek to engender a sense of optimism and to reappraise Chinese futures, especially when relating to socio-political visions, and to the current practices in Chinese urban design and architecture that take so little of humanity into account.

'If I could think what I would do, other than architecture, it would be to write the new fairy tale, because from the fairy tale came the airplane, and the locomotive, and the wonderful instruments of our minds... it all came from wonder.' – Louis I. Kahn[10]

COMICS AND ITS POLITICAL IDENTITY

A city is an ongoing rehearsal of spatial choreographies influenced by many determining factors including political ideologies; and by the same token, comics is a palimpsest of how we act, think, fear and dream collectively. When 'pen is put to paper', narratives are written and re-written, cities are born and reborn, whether by the hand of the master architect, the visionary monarch, or the imaginative author. It is not just the great novels and treatises that inspire political engagement of the everyday citizen; the ephemeral commentaries of political satire and humorous imagery can communicate instantly and effectively. There exists a long history of comics shifting perspectives to reinforce power and ideas, a history that can be found in cultures from all over the world. The history of the modern-Western comics began in America around 1900; this is a definitive moment where the essential qualities of the medium become 'inseparably tied to the notion of the city'.[11] In the Chinese context, the illustrated scrolls with calligraphy eventually led to 'Manhua' (impromptu sketches) and the 'big-character posters' of the 19th and 20th centuries.

The tradition of storytelling with comic-like illustrations dates from the Western Han dynasty. Pictures of heroes have been found displayed on walls, and carved into stones all throughout ancient times. John A. Lent and Xu Ying, authors of 'Comics Art in China' (2017), explained that 'for centuries, Chinese painters poked fun at the social and political systems under which they worked. As with artists of dissent in similar circumstances, they veiled their meanings',[12] and related the golden ages in cartooning to the days where political and social life were deeply fraught. The relationship between the citizen and the political systems has played out even more prominently in the comics of the last few hundred years. 'The unsettling and turbulent times were ripe for cartoonists, whose vitriol spewed out towards such a multitude of targets... humour was now considered an indispensable element of modernity.'[13]

Mao Zedong exploited comic-like illustrations for political gains – the Communist Party of China quickly grabbed onto the strategy of using cartoons with simple slogans to produce widespread, speedy and effective weapons of propaganda and war. The printed image can deal a shocking and emotive blow to the reader; in a few attention-grabbing seconds it can communicate and manipulate before the readers have time to consult their own thoughts or misconceptions on the matter. This form of graphical communication is ephemeral enough, fast enough and ambiguous enough to deliver political and ideological critique (and perhaps consequential urban change) to a wide, and perhaps quite inattentive, audience. For architects, comics is a powerful tool to instil their design with a socio-political position – be that of influence, awareness or even defiance (innovation). While the golden age of Manhua had been in the 1920s and 30s, the period that followed Mao's death in 1976 was the highest point of freedom of expression, a time where printed cartoons and comics were employed to criticise government propaganda.[14]

In recent times, Manhua no longer relies on the printed media. With readily available social media and online publication, technology has offered unlimited opportunities for political animators and cartoonists. Comics, like other forms of cartoons and animations, has become increasingly digitised, and there are concerns that the exciting territory and the temptation of the three-dimensional is perhaps undermining some of the clarity of expression. Lent and

Xu argue that three-dimensional and vector-graphics are often 'too additive – too detailed – in an art form that traditionally reduced things to their essentials'; they feel that the tools could marginalise political comic illustrators when trying to hold a critical thinking position within a larger theme, or when dealing with complex softwares.[15] Yet we must work within our era - and so we embrace the contrary, mindful that digitisation has offered the comic-inspired drawings in this book the benefit of multidisciplinary and critical engagements with diverse aesthetic interactions between humans and the built environment in a literary, poetic or philosophical manner. Together, the two-dimensional analogue-made marks with the digitally aided three-dimensional layers retain the tension and nuance of a traditionally assembled collage.

As architects and designers, we are familiar and dexterous with tools which blur the distinction between reality and fiction. 'Rem Koolhaas in his proposal for Euralille in the 90s, used the language of comics to get his idea of hyper-modernism across. To ensure that people (and the government) would understand and be able to identify themselves with a very conceptual project, the networked city, he didn't use floor plans, elevations or perspectives. Instead he adopted the language of comics', argued Francois Rambert, co-curator of the comics exhibition 'Archi et BD, la ville dessinée'

(2010).[16] Even with Koolhaas's appeal for historic preservation of the Beijing Hutongs lending the architect a noble and considerate side to his reputation, there is a characterisation in 'Batman: Death by design' (2013) of 'an affected, narcissistic genius' Netherlandish master builder named Kem Roomhaus. The threat of Roomhaus and his techno-utopian, competition-winning proposals is finally ended by Batman and his alter-ego Bruce Wayne. The DC Comics' graphic novel by Chip Kidd and Dave Taylor is a cautionary tale of corruption and architectural hubris highlighting the detrimental effects on civic culture of architectural destruction in Gotham City, but could equally be set in any Chinese city.

In the history of comics and the city, 'Amazing Archigram / Zoom' (1964) deconstructed the comic superhero, discovered modernity and became the stimulus for much of the heroic era of visionary architecture of the 60s and 70s. Archigram reinvented architecture for the age of the consumer by using bold comics language with speech bubbles and onomatopoeias, enriched with references to graphic narratives, Pop Art imagery, advertising and technology. The anthropologist and author Mélanie van der Hoorn also recognises the ability of comics to question contemporary society and identity: '...often dismissed as a light-footed, low-threshold form of amusement, but perhaps it is exactly for this reason that comics functions as a wolf in sheep's clothing, bringing serious and critical remarks in an unobtrusive way.'[17] The colourful four-page comic strip 'Metaperlach: The strip on the end of planning tyranny and the beginning of democratic process planning' (1969), famously derided bureaucracy and those who followed rules and prescriptions blindly when designing.

Might architecture be more accessible if they are designed as responsive satires? Following a similar line of enquiry, MVRDV's Comic and Animation Museum in Hangzhou attempts to bring comics to life in a three-dimensional interpretation of the two-dimensional speech bubble motif. Perhaps every city should have a comics store – a forum to bring together environmental, social and political protagonists from opposing positions. Comics and bookstores, immersed with their own beguiling stories, serve as sanctuaries and 'should provide space, vision and nurture the city with its humanitarian spirit. It's a place for people to have dreams in the city'[18] declared Qian Xiaohua, the owner of Nanjing's Librairie Avant-Garde located beneath Wutaishan Stadium, inside a former government underground parking lot once used as a bomb shelter. While the massive 4000-square-metre Nanjing outlet is perceived to be a 'spiritual guide', Ou Ning's Librairie Avant-Garde in Bishan village – in a former cowshed converted from a local clan ancestral hall surrounded by rice paddies – is a call for a renewed relationship with the countryside and economic revitalisation without resorting to industrialisation. The social experiment echoes the complementary infiltration of Archigram's comic-strip Instant City (1968).

There is increased awareness of unsustainable environmental and unethical social practices, partly attributed to storytellers in the mass media. Science provides statistical proof that humanity is both perpetrator and victim, but statistical abstraction fails to engage the public imagination in the way story-shaped issues can. Over the following chapters, we will delve into China's literature, myths, hear-says, political propaganda and dissident poetry; the act of interrogation is required to draw from diverse contexts to determine China's built environmental futures. The populist, economic, political and historic stories of the world's most populous country are immensely fertile resources from which to speculate new architectural imaginations through the ideas of representation and the potential of the hybrid text-and-image medium of comics.

CHINESE TRAJECTORIES

China was once the epitome of civilisation. And led by different ideologies and aspirations over the centuries, the nation along with its comics art has reincarnated time and time again. Chinese comics has actively engaged in the years of socio-political dissatisfaction with national government and colonial or other interfering foreign nations. So often the wings of progress cast shadows of exploitation, the strength of riches threatens democracy and equality, and the corruption of power facilitates a reputation of greed and suspicion. But still China surges ahead.

In 'Understanding the Chinese City' (2014), Li Shiqiao identifies '... the overwhelming expansion of Chinese cities today and the viable economic life they accommodate that brought a pressing need for theory. The unexpected but compelling development of Chinese cities since the 1980s have aroused tremendous attention outside the relative confines of sinology; there is a genuine sense that what is taking place in China could indeed become a common but unfamiliar future.'[19] There is the need for, and the reality of, new social interpretations and imaginative spatial politics, and it is in this arena that we situate the chapters of 'Once Upon a China' – for the benefit of the joint endeavours of local and foreign interpreters and agents of change, who will determine the next era for China.

Mao Zedong's 'Great Leap Forward' campaign led the nation into a tumultuous period in the late 1950s and early 60s. The radical social system swiftly relinquished power to Deng Xiaoping's economic reforms, which unleashed China's economic boom and capitalist ambitions. The 'opening of China' has affected all areas of life, and one of the beneficiaries is the built environment – China has since been building cities at a rate of knots. The state has ushered in a massive construction boom that has achieved what seems like astronomic progress to some, and to others this vast consumption of resources has left unforgiveable waste and terrifying environmental damage. The expansion of generic and expedited construction styles has torn huge gaps in historical urban fabric, with local communities pushed out of their home cities and replaced by those drawn by the magnet of commerce. Grand architectural gestures such as those for the 2008 Beijing Olympics have had massive political emphasis, but in many cases the aspirations were poorly constructed, while icons designed for once-in-a-lifetime sporting events lay dormant and almost completely misused.

At the time of writing, China's population is estimated at around 1.4 billion and is equivalent to 18.59 per cent of the world's total population according to the United Nations Population Data. Despite innumerable new 'instant cities' built across the country, these 'mathematical model' cities, complete with housing, cultural centres and civic spaces, lack inhabitants apart from the employees of government institutions. The critical mass of Chinese migrants from rural areas remains captivated by the megacities such as Beijing, Chongqing, Guangzhou, Shanghai and Shenzhen. Beijing, as observed by NASA's Jet Propulsion Laboratory, had already quadrupled in size between 1999 and 2009[20] before announcing that in coming years, the capital will be further transformed and grow the metropolitan zone to around six times that of New York. 'Beijing is the most inhuman city that I have ever lived in, even among Chinese cities. Of course, there's nothing wrong with this. Since we are an inhuman society, we should have an inhuman city',[21] lamented Ai Weiwei, the celebrated Chinese political artist.

It is a sad and frustrating set of affairs, to consider that the country's recovery from a cultural revolution may not really include all that much re-investment in 'real' culture. The capitalist system seems so antagonistic and the business world so treacherous, that the quality of heritage, literature, art and storytelling is almost completely missing, or confined to the shadows. What remains, apart from the pastiche, is a cynical commercial antiquities platform, where artefacts are judged to be an attractive currency to store wealth. Those same private investors and custodians serve what they believe to be a patriotic duty, to carefully protect and invest in the treasures of cultural history while operating under high risk, especially in a market where the authentic and the replica are difficult to determine.[22] With ever more global challenges facing China, now far-outgrown of its adolescent stage, interrogation can be made into how historical and cultural approaches in design speculation might offer clues for alternative spatial models.

Historically, the operations and consequences of Chinese domesticity, consumerism, democracy and adaptability have often received criticism from the West. Before the 2008 Olympics, severe traffic controls and temporary closures of factories and power stations were imposed in Beijing and its surrounding areas as the city was required to improve air quality for over half a million tourists and sports fans visiting.[23] In December 2015, Beijing issued the first ever air pollution 'Red Alert'[24] – smog has served as an uncomfortable warning that the country's existing manufacturing and coal-fired energy production are threats to future generations.

Nevertheless, China remains critical to the global clean energy story as Climatescope 2020 reported, 'China and India continue to be the biggest markets for clean energy investment with China far and away the largest. Between them, the two nations accounted for $94 billion of new wind/solar investment and 76GW of wind/solar build in 2019. China led the world with 62GW of wind/solar added. India built 14GW.'[25] While renewables provide significant economic growth opportunities and the Chinese are likely to continue in that vein, 'China, to be clear, is still the world's largest emitter of greenhouse gases, and it doesn't plan to peak its emissions until 2030. But its early commitment to clean energy means it can continue its rapid rate of growth with far less pollution than it would produce otherwise.'[26]

China's urbanisation also faces other complications, as a result of the country's 'one-child policy' and increased life expectancies; the threat of a 4-2-1 family will play heavily on the minds of the young. When economic migrants of working age move to cities, they leave behind two generations of elderly, but continue to have the traditional responsibility to provide financial security for the parents and sometimes four grandparents. Furthermore, the country's workforce is beginning to diminish as a percentage of the whole, and with it comes the shrinkage in the country's capacity as the world's factory. There have been predictions that by 2030, China will have to import workers from outside its borders rather than exporting them. 'In the absence of predictable institutions, all areas of Chinese society have relied on guanxi, the web of connections that often has extended family relations at the centre. But what happens when there are fewer extended families? One result could be a move towards a more predictable legal system and (possibly) a more open political culture.'[27] As of 2016, the national birth planning policy became a universal 'two-child policy' per family.

Society is changing, energy consumption needs changing, and together with the changing climate, China's resilience depends on being a fully connected society, and on reimagining relationships between globalisation and localisation, amongst individuals as well as governments and corporate decision-makers. The future of Chinese urbanism and architecture will be radical, but should learn from the mistakes of the past, from the laboratory-cities of the West, and perhaps from the virtues of its own identity and stories – without first being wiped clean. And if the rest of the world wants to connect with China, to work together across borders and mindsets, we have to know each other's stories. Former US President Barack Obama advocates: 'If you know someone, if you've talked to them face-to-face, if you can forge a connection, you may not agree with them on everything, but there's some common ground to be found, and you can move forward together. We want people to be able to get outside of themselves and experience and understand the lives of somebody else, which is what a good story does. It helps all of us feel some sort of solidarity with each other.'[28]

NOTES

1. WW Ai, 'Weiwei-isms', Larry Walsh (ed.), Princeton University Press, 2013, p.43

2. N Ou, 'The China Issue', ICON magazine, James McLachlan (ed.), March 2018, p.73

3. Xinhua News Agency, 'Chinese "Muggles" Meet Harry Potter Together with the World', China Daily, 21 July 2007 [http://www.chinadaily.com.cn/china/2007-07/21/content_5440958.htm], retrieved 11 February 2018

4. H Yu, 'China in Ten Words', AH Barr (trans.), Anchor Books, New York, 2011, p.55

5. WLY Yang & CP Adkins, 'Critical Essays on Chinese Fiction', The Chinese University of Hong Kong, 1980, p.1

6. WLY Yang & CP Adkins, 'Critical Essays on Chinese Fiction', The Chinese University of Hong Kong, 1980, pp.xii–xiv

7. JA Lent & Y Xu, 'Comics Art in China', University Press of Mississippi, 2017, p.24

8. J Ahrens & A Meteling (eds.), 'Comics and the City: Urban space in print, picture and sequence', Continuum, London, 2010, p.5

9. J Ahrens & A Meteling (eds.), 'Comics and the City: Urban space in print, picture and sequence', Continuum, London 2010, p.9

10. LI Khan, 'Conversations with Students' (second edition), Rice University School of Architecture and Princeton Architectural Press, Houston, 1998, p.15

11. J Ahrens & A Meteling (eds.), 'Comics and the City: Urban space in print, picture and sequence', Continuum, London 2010, p.4

12. JA Lent & Y Xu, 'Comics Art in China', University Press of Mississippi, 2017, pp.4–6

13+14. JA Lent & Y Xu, 'Comics Art in China', University Press of Mississippi, 2017, p.23

15. JA Lent & Y Xu, 'Comics Art in China', University Press of Mississippi, 2017, p.192

16. E Sommariva, 'The City in the Comics', Domus, 16 June 2010 [https://www.
domusweb.it/en/architecture/2010/06/16/the-city-in-the-comics.html], retrieved 11
March 2018

17. M van der Hoorn, 'Bricks & Balloons: Architecture in comic-strip form', 010
Publishers, Rotterdam, 2012, p.96

18. F Cha, 'Bookmark This! World's Best Bookstores', CNN: Travel, 4 August 2015 [http://
edition.cnn.com/travel/article/worlds-coolest-bookstores-new/index.html], retrieved 11
March 2018

19. SQ Li, 'Understanding the Chinese City', SAGE Publications, London, 2014, p.xxii

20. NASA Earth Science News Team, 'Beijing Quadrupled in Size in a Decade', NASA
Finds, 5 June 2015 [https://www.nasa.gov/jpl/beijing-quadrupled-in-size-in-a-decade-
nasa-finds], retrieved 7 January 2021

21. WW Ai, 'Ai Weiwei Speaks: With Hans Ulrich Obrist', Penguin Books, 2011, p.34

22. N Collins, 'Rise of the Chinese Antiques Market', The Telegraph, 10 November 2010

23. J Yardley, 'Beijing's Olympic Quest: Turn smoggy sky blue', The New York Times, 29
December 2007

24. BBC News, 'China pollution: First ever red alert in effect in Beijing', 7 December 2015
[https://www.bbc.co.uk/news/world-asia-china-35026363], retrieved 6 January 2021

25. Climatescope, 'Emerging Markets Outlook 2020: Energy transition in the world's
fastest growing economies', Bloomberg NEF, 9 December 2020, p.3

26. T McDonnell, 'China Is Absolutely Destroying the US on Clean Energy', Mother
Jones, 24 November 2015 [http://www.motherjones.com/blue-marble/2015/11/china-
absolutely-destroying-us-clean-energy], retrieved 3 December 2015

27. The Economist, 'China's Achilles Heel', 21 April 2012 [http://www.economist.com/
node/21553056], retrieved 3 December 2015

28. B Obama, 'American Factory: A short conversation with the Obamas', Netflix, 2019